SIMPLICITY NOW

SIMPLICITY
NOW

60 WAYS TO EXPERIENCE JOYFUL SIMPLICITY

ST. MARTIN'S
ESSENTIALS
NEW YORK

JESSE SANDS

First published in the United States by St. Martin's Essentials, an imprint of
St. Martin's Publishing Group

www.stmartins.com

Design by Jonathan Bennett

Library of Congress Cataloging-in-Publication Data

Names: Sands, Jesse, author.
Title: Simplicity now : 60 ways to experience joyful simplicity /
    Jesse Sands.
Description: First Edition. | New York : St. Martin's Essentials, 2020. |
    Series: The now series
Identifiers: LCCN 2020024204 | ISBN 9781250765505 (trade
    paperback) | ISBN 9781250765512 (ebook)
Subjects: LCSH: Self-help techniques. | Simplicity.
Classification: LCC BF632 .S26 2020 | DDC 158—dc23
LC record available at https://lccn.loc.gov/2020024204

Our books may be purchased in bulk for promotional, educational,
or business use. Please contact your local bookseller or the Macmillan
Corporate and Premium Sales Department at 1-800-221-7945, extension 5442,
or by email at MacmillanSpecialMarkets@macmillan.com.

First Edition: 2020

10 9 8 7 6 5 4 3 2 1

The most simple things can bring
the most happiness.

—IZABELLA SCORUPCO

SIMPLICITY NOW

INTRODUCTION

Years ago I was in a tough place in my life. I was broke, alone, and unhealthy, both physically and mentally. It was a dark period. When things were at their worst, I felt forced to make changes; it was either change or stay in pain. I began readjusting my attitude and rethinking many of my decisions. I worked to make happiness and abundance priorities in my life. I began to meditate and learned about mindfulness.

All of these positive changes had one very unexpected side effect: I wanted less. Less "stuff." Less drama. Less negativity. Less pain. Less of everything that kept me small and hurt and hidden.

As I tried to untangle the mess that my life seemed to have become, I found that I craved the opposite of mess, the opposite of complicated: I craved simplicity. Simple finances, meaning making more than I spend and having savings (and eventually, investments). Simple relationships, meaning ones based on love and respect. A simple home, meaning having only those possessions that create happiness. Simple health, meaning eating less bad stuff, eating more good stuff, drinking more water, and moving more.

This is important: simple doesn't mean easy. It also doesn't mean stupid. Those are two synonyms for the word "simple," but they aren't the ones I mean when I use it. I mean uncomplicated. Life is complicated enough on its own; there's no reason to make it more so. I found that I was making choices and indulging in behaviors that weren't in my best interest. Simplicity meant, for me, making decisions that made my life easier and better.

Bit by bit, my life began to get a little less complicated. Of course, I wanted it to happen fast—like tomorrow! But it had taken me years to get my life in the messy state it was in, so I needed to realize that it would take me some weeks, months, and even years for me to create a life that was in alignment with my goals.

Some things did change quickly. I took on the easy tasks first, clearing out drawers and closets. It felt good to live with more organization. That spurred me to do more. The deeper untangling took longer. I kept at it consistently, and change did happen. But there are still corners of my life I'm working on tidying.

In this book, I've collected the wisdom I learned and the methods I used. I don't mean to tell you that I have all the answers and there's nothing more for me to learn—of course not! What I can tell you, though, is that the simpler I make things, the more meaningful those things become.

Simplicity can be applied to every area of your life. It's very popular right now to think of simplifying your life by organizing your house and office. That's a great way to begin. Surrounding yourself with space and organization will definitely have a positive effect on your life. You can then take this idea into other areas as well.

Remember, though, that simplicity isn't only about what's around you; it also refers to what's inside you. Simplicity in your body, simplicity in your mind, and simplicity in your actions will create positive change in your life. You can achieve this change by making simplicity a priority, one of the values that you work at every day.

I've learned that, contrary to what our consumer culture would have you believe, less is more. Simplicity is decluttering every part of your life (not just your house). In that decluttering, you create space. And in that space, you will find freedom.

THE SIMPLICITY MANIFESTO

I value simplicity in my life. I choose order and organization over clutter and mess. I say what I mean, and mean what I say. Simplicity brings space to my mind, my body, and my surroundings. Space is freedom. Less is more. Quality over quantity. All is well.

LETTING GO

The hardest part of simplifying your life might just be the act of letting go. After all, the "things" we hold on to—whether they are actual physical things, or grudges, or feelings—are connections to memories of the past, good or bad. "Things" represent our lives.

To let go, we sometimes worry, means we are forgetting the past. But the opposite is actually true. The more we let go of, the more space we have—literally and figuratively—to remember what is meaningful.

Life is really simple, but
we insist on making it
complicated.

—CONFUCIUS

Try This—Use What You Have

Go through your house, into your cupboards or drawers, and find two or three (or more) items that you have never used or haven't used in a long time. Now, use them.

If you find that these items are no longer needed or wanted, then pass them along. Same with clothes. What clothes are in your closet that you aren't wearing? Pull them out, and either begin to wear them or donate them. Use what you have . . . otherwise, why have it?

KEEP VALUE

One popular organizer says that we should hold each object that we own, and keep only those that bring us joy. That's true, but I would also add that you should keep objects that have value, at least to you. There are many kinds of value, including financial, emotional, and familial. If what you own doesn't have value, it's robbing you of time and energy.

Try This—The 10 Items

Here is a great question that you can answer yourself or bring up with friends over dinner. If you had to live on a desert island and could take only ten items with you, what would they be?

You can set parameters on this question, such as considering only non-clothing or nonfood items, but the point is to think of what your ten most essential possessions are.

The greatest wealth is to live
content with little.

—PLATO

LOVING LESS

We live in a "more, more, more" society. Ads, television shows, movies all show depictions of people buying, shopping, wanting more, buying more. If one car is good, three is better, and why not have five? If a three-bedroom house is nice, why not upgrade to a seven-bedroom house, each with en suite.

For some people, it's a medal of honor to have dozens of pairs of shoes, or multiple expensive watches, or more of anything. But ask yourself this: How much is enough? Is it better to have more or to love what you already have? And let's really get to the deep truth . . . Don't you already have more than enough in several areas of your life? More stuff is suffocating, not liberating.

If that's too difficult, try to narrow it down—what ten books from your collection would you take to a desert island if you could bring only ten? What ten pieces of clothing? And so on. This will help you prioritize what you have, what you need, and what you can get rid of.

Try This—Reusing in New Ways

Sometimes I think of the sheer number of bottles—both glass and plastic—that people use and discard every single day. What happens to all of those empty bottles? How do they effect the planet?

If you do an internet search, you will find a variety of information about where bottles (and other trash) go when we're done with them. In my quest to make my life as simple as possible, I've decided to reuse bottles when I can, in as many ways as I can.

There's a store nearby where I can refill hand soap, shampoo, dish soap, and more. I clean water bottles I've used, and reuse them over and over. I've used bottles as vases, decorations, coin banks, and everything else

I can think of. I certainly don't reuse them all, but it's easier than you think to reuse something as simple as a bottle.

YOU CAN'T TAKE IT WITH YOU

Have you heard the cliché "You can't take it with you"? Well, like many clichés, it happens to reveal a truth. Our lives are short. Have you noticed how fast the time goes? As I write this, it's almost Christmas, but it feels like just yesterday that the year started.

As the famous song goes, we all think we have more time until we don't. I truly believe that at the end I won't regret not having had more shoes, more money in the bank, a big house. I will be glad for all the people I loved well and I'll be proud of the good person I tried to become and of everything I gave back to those I loved and to the world. That's it.

"Stuff" is complicated. Love and giving are simple.

It is the sweet, simple things
of life which are the real
ones after all.

—LAURA INGALLS WILDER

Try This—5 Items a Day

A couple of times a year I do a "quick cleanse." I grab a couple of big bags and set them out. Then, every day for a week, I walk around the house and look for five things that I could easily get rid of and place them in a bag.

At the end of the week, I drop off my bag(s) at a charity store. In one week, I get rid of thirty-five things that I no longer want and that others can use. It's easy, fast, and virtually effortless. I'm always amazed at how easy it is to find things to get rid of. Why keep them? Less is more.

MORE SPACE

This is one of my mantras: Space equals freedom. Another one is: Less is more. They seem like paradoxes, but like all Zen paradoxes, they contain a lot of truth.

Clutter in my thoughts means I have less space for creativity, imagination, forgiveness, and passion. Clutter in my house means I have less space to expand, less ability to relax. Clutter in my relationships means I get caught up in drama. No more clutter, internally or externally.

Try This—Make a List of Experiences Rather Than Possessions

Make a list of experiences that you would like to have in the next six months (or year, or any time frame that you choose).

This could be traveling to new places. It could also be something creative, like visiting a museum in your city on its "free day." Or walking through every park in your area, or cooking as many dishes as you can using only what you already have in your kitchen, or . . . The idea is to have fun and enjoy experiences instead of objects.

START WITH ONE DRAWER

Sometimes the clutter of life can feel over-whelming. Many of us carry so much in our lives. So keeping in mind the rule of simplicity, just start with one thing.

Pick one drawer. You know the drawer . . . the one where you stuff everything, the drawer that is the "catchall" for all your junk. Clean it, and make it work for you rather than just being a place you cram things. Just one drawer. How long would that take? Ten minutes? A half hour max? Start there. See how it makes you feel.

Hold to these principles: seek simplicity, grasp the essential, overcome selfishness and wasteful desires.

—**TAO TE CHING**

Try This—Make Gifts, Don't Buy Them

How amazing would it be if this year, rather than buying something new, you gave gifts that you made or that you repurposed from what you already own?

If you're like me, you have beautiful items others have gifted to you that you don't really want, and that you can regift to others. (Just remember to not regift the item back to the person who gifted it to you in the first place!) If you put some thought into it, I predict, your friends and family members will love the personal touch that you put into your gift to them.

11 QUICK WAYS TO LIVE SIMPLY

Say no when you mean no, and yes when you mean yes.

Unsubscribe to as many emails as possible.

Turn off the television.

Clean a drawer, or a closet, or your garage.

Eat simple food, slowly.

Drink more water.

Give something away each day for a week.

Meditate.

Do one thing at a time
—don't multitask.

Use as little plastic as possible.

Reuse bottles, bags, and other items
as often as you can.

GIVE TO RECEIVE

Here's a cool thing to remember. Giving to others blesses you back. When you give from your overflow, you actually receive. What do you receive? You receive joy, you receive gratitude for how much you've given, and you receive more space. And remember, space equals . . . what? Freedom!

As you begin to create more space in your house and your office, give away what no longer serves you, or the things that you don't love. In giving them to others you are gaining so much more.

Try This—Pass It On

Walk around your home and find five things you can give to important people in your life. You can either pick the five items and then think of who you can give them to, or you can think of five people and pick specific items for each of them.

Don't give them stuff just to get rid of it—put some thought and effort into it. Giving away something from your home is giving a little bit of yourself to the people closest to you.

BREATHE EASY

I found that the more stuff I had, the less deeply I was able to breathe. Every room in my house was filled with stuff. Every drawer, every closet. My garage. My kitchen counters, my refrigerator. All of it demanded upkeep, cleaning, time, and energy.

So which came first: breathing deeply or getting rid of "stuff"? I'm not sure, but I do know that the less stuff I had the more I was able to breathe, and that the more deeply I breathed the less I felt the need to have things. There's a powerful connection between our vitality of life and how much openness we allow ourselves.

Try This—Simple Life, Happy Life

Have you heard the phrase "Happy wife, happy life"? Well, I don't know about that, but what I can speak to is a variation on that theme: simple life, happy life.

How can you simplify your life starting today, or this week? Make a list of ways that come to mind, and then pick two or three and begin doing them. Simple life means living simply and simply living.

The best things in life
aren't things.

—ART BUCHWALD

HAPPINESS ISN'T IN THE "THINGS"

I used to watch this reality show where there was a rich lady who had a bunch of rich friends, and they talked about their riches and bought expensive things. Don't ask me why I watched it—or why millions of others did, too! Anyway, the husband of this rich lady died unexpectedly. Suddenly, she was in real pain.

What helped her? In fact, what *saved* her? It wasn't the houses, the clothes, the money. It was her friends. Today, you wouldn't think this woman is the same one from the show. She looks different now, lighter. She doesn't seem to be consumed by "things" anymore; she realizes that happiness is in our experiences, not our stuff.

Try This—Seeing Your Space Through a Stranger's Eyes

Go outside your front door and take a few breaths. Then, come back into your house and pretend as if you've never seen it before. Notice your space the way, say, a real estate agent might. Take note of the walls, the paint, how many items there are around, the condition of everything.

What improvements do you need to make? What areas look crowded or cluttered? What is missing? We get so used to the space we live in that we don't see it the way it really is. Seeing your space with new eyes makes your next steps simple.

GIFT-GIVING NOW

Make this your goal. Go through your house and find things that you either won't miss or that no longer serve you. Then find ways to give those things to others. You can gift them to other people, or take them to a charity, or put them on the curb for others to take.

Whatever you get rid of in order to create more space in your life can also bless others. There

is a cliché that says, "One man's junk is another man's treasure." I won't call it "junk," but
I will say that when I've given things to others
who value them, we both get a gift.

Try This—Homemade Gift Wrap

I went to a museum with a friend, and as we walked up to the front counter to get our tickets we noticed a display of free maps of the museum. My friend took two or three of them, and I asked her why she was taking more than one.

She told me that in order to be more environmentally friendly, she doesn't usually gift wrap many gifts anymore, but that when she does she uses free maps like these. Her friends and family love it, she said, and it's a way to promote the museums as well.

I should mention that she took only two or three, not a dozen. Thinking of creative ways to reuse items is simple, sweet, and meaningful, all at the same time.

BEING THE CHANGE,
SETTING THE EXAMPLE

As you create emotional and physical space in your life, you will notice your mood changing. You will notice the way you walk through the world changing. As you notice it, others will as well. You may even be asked, "What are you doing? Why are you so happy?"

By simplifying, you will be creating an example for other people, even without intending to. Isn't it good to know that as you create more space and freedom in your life, you are being a catalyst to inspire others to do the same?

Try This—Holiday List
Think of your birthday and holiday list and to whom you plan on giving gifts. Start considering what gifts you can give that will reflect your value of simplicity.

For example, a friend of mine once wrote each of his closest friends and family members a short story in which they were the main character. He spent months working on them, and it showed. Everyone loved them, and I still have mine. What can you do that reflects you and your feelings for each person, but isn't just another factory-made item?

USE WHAT YOU HAVE

I bought a toaster. The thing is, I already had a toaster that worked. Why did I buy the new toaster? I asked myself that when I came home.

My immediate answer was that I bought the new one because it was fancier than the toaster that I already had. If my old toaster didn't work, that would be one thing, but it did work. So why did I need to buy a new one? I didn't.

What are some "toasters" in your life? The things that are perfectly functional that you have become discontented with? Can you learn to appreciate what you have without adding more things to your life?

Try This—Simplicity List

Are there any parts of your life that feel complicated? Finances? Health? Relationships? Work? Something else?

Make a list of whatever areas in your life feel more complicated than you'd like them to. Now, next to each thing, write down one or two things you could do immediately that would help to make the complicated a little simpler.

Repeat this exercise as often as needed, whether daily, weekly, monthly, or yearly.

Simple can be harder than complex. You have to work hard to get your thinking clean to make it simple. But it's worth it in the end because once you get there, you can move mountains.

—STEVE JOBS

SIMPLIFYING IS NOT EASY

Simplifying, both externally and internally, is hard. Well, some of it is easy, but much of it is difficult. We can attribute all kinds of meaning to objects.

Whether we think they hold memories or are proof of our socioeconomic status or represent a fantasy version of our lives, we place all kinds of emotional value on objects that prevents us from seeing them for the burden they are.

Decluttering is hard work, because it requires us to confront these emotional connections and resolve them before we can even touch the physical objects.

Try This—Goodwill Challenge

Pick a nonprofit organization such as Goodwill (do some research before choosing the place, and call to make sure it's accepting donations). Imagine how much good work the organization does. Wouldn't it feel great to help support their work?

Here's the challenge: time yourself for one hour, and find as many things as you can to donate to that nonprofit. Bag it up neatly, then call the nonprofit to arrange for a pickup (or drop it off on your own). By doing this you will be helping others and helping yourself. And all it took was one hour.

THE 3 QUESTIONS

I worked for two years with an organizing coach. Yes, two years! She began our time together by saying that we were going to spend our time literally touching everything I owned, and asking the same question for each item.

The question was: Is this to keep? Or to donate? Or to trash? And if the answer was "To keep," she would ask, "Why?" This forced me to be clear about each and every object I owned, and about why I kept it. It was startling. When we got to my three cheese graters, I saw her point.

If you cannot explain it simply, you don't understand it well enough.

—ALBERT EINSTEIN

Try This—Photographs

If you have a lot of photographs—especially old family ones—and they are disorganized in a box or drawer, try this.

Set aside some time and space. Look at each photo and put it in a specific pile by category. Categories could include: photos of you, photos of those you know, photos of those you don't recognize, photos that have no value (blurry, etc.). For the pile with people you don't recognize, ask other family members if they can identify them.

Once you have everything in piles, go through each pile to determine which photos you want to keep, which you can give to relatives, and which you can discard. The photos you keep, place in chronological order, then put in albums. The photos you give away, give away soon. And discard the rest. You will value your photographs now more than ever before.

ORGANIZED, NOT CRAZED

When I first began to declutter my home and my mind, I went crazy with it. I was throwing things out left and right, trying to keep as little as possible. The problem was, I was throwing away (or donating) things that I actually needed, just to throw yet another thing out of the house.

I went overboard. My heart was in the right place, but I made it a competitive thing, trying to be the best-organized person ever. Gradually I realized that I just needed to be clear. If I liked it, if it had meaning, if I used it, then it stayed. That was enough.

Try This—Waste Less Water

It's astounding to think that there are areas in the world where people do not have access to clean water. And even in some large cities, there are strict water restrictions due to the lack of available usable water. It's frustrating to read about these situations, and sometimes I feel so powerless.

However, I've decided to do what I can to help. I take short showers, use "gray water" to water my plants, make sure I have a full load before running the dishwasher or washing machine, turn off the bathroom faucet while I brush my teeth, and do everything else I can think of to conserve water.

I don't know how much effect I can have as one person, but I do know that it contributes a little, and that if millions of people were to take some of these steps, it would have a big impact.

Never overlook
the power of simplicity.

—ROBIN S. SHARMA

5 SIMPLE LIFE DECISIONS

I now value simple over complicated in all areas of my life.

I choose to align my thoughts, words, and actions.

I now choose quality over quantity.

I go to bed early, and wake up early.

I am deliberate in my outer and inner world.

HOW MANY PENS
(I COUNTED SIXTY-THREE . . .)

When I cleaned out my office, I got to my pens. I had a plastic container filled with pens that I had collected over the years. I always held on to them, because I hated that feeling of needing a pen and not being able to find one. However, when I took out that container and counted them, I had to wonder what on earth I would do with sixty-three pens.

I needed only a few of my favorite ones, and perhaps one red-ink one; the rest could go. At first I didn't want to get rid of them—after all, perhaps someday I might . . . But I knew they could be used by other people *now*, and if I needed more pens later, I could buy them.

I took fifty-seven pens to my church and set them out so people who needed an extra pen or two could take one. They were gone in about ten minutes. And me? I felt lighter, and haven't missed them even once since. And that was just pens! I soon took the same approach to many other "things" as well.

Try This—Simplicity in Social Media

Have you noticed that people who use social media like to provide a running commentary on their lives? Their social media streams are filled with every one of their thoughts and emotions and opinions and actions and reactions.

It's absolutely their right to make that choice. However, when I decided to value simplicity, I also made the decision to post only truly meaningful things. Before posting anything, I wait at least an hour (and usually a day) so I'm certain it's authentically me. There's enough noise on social media without me adding to it.

TRAVEL LIGHT

The Buddha said that it's best to travel light. Those weren't his words, but throughout his teachings, he warns against attachment to "things." When we are attached to anything, be it a possession or a belief, we become imprisoned by it.

However, when we hold things lightly, we get the benefit of them without being tied to them. In this way, we aren't weighted down or limited by anything. When we travel lightly through life, we can go farther.

Try This—Turn Off the Television

If you want to take the advanced course in creating a simple life, try doing the most revolutionary thing there is—turn off your television for an entire month.

If that's too much for you, try it for a whole week, or even a whole day. At first it'll feel extremely difficult to shut off that rectangle in your living room (or wherever you put it), but once you do, you'll find that it yields amazing benefits. You'll have more energy, and find more time to do things like reading, writing, painting, and spending time with your family.

LEARNING FROM OTHERS

When her only living parent died, one of my friends had to clean out her parents' house. It was an arduous task, clearly filled with great sorrow. What made the experience even more difficult was how many possessions her parents had amassed.

Her mother had not thrown out much over the years, and there were boxes and containers and closets packed with items from the parents' lives. The garage was filled, and my friend discovered there was also a storage unit filled with things from her childhood, old furniture, and more.

My friend vowed then and there to go through her own stuff, clear it out, and organize whatever was left so that her children wouldn't have to endure what she did. It's a gift that she can give her children, plus it'll benefit her life now.

Try This—Simplicity in Style, in Word, in Action

Simplicity isn't just about organizing, decluttering, and using less. It is also about being more deliberate in your words and your actions. Being clear in what we say and what we do creates a simplicity in our lifestyle as well.

If you say positive things, and do positive things, you tend to create more positive experiences. That's a simple equation that anyone can follow. But first you must be willing to give up negativity and drama.

SWEDISH DEATH CLEANING

My friend discovered for herself that her parents' things could become a burden, but there's actually an entire tradition built around the practice of cleaning *before* death.

The Swedish tradition, *döstädning,* essentially means "death cleaning." It's the practice of cleaning out your possessions now, while you are alive. The idea is to prevent your family and friends from having to sort through your possessions after your death. You can enlist your family and friends to help, and it becomes a bonding experience.

It might sound morbid, but it's actually kindness in action. It will help you now, and it will help them later.

With wisdom comes the
desire for simplicity.

—**BRENDON BURCHARD**

Try This—Read the Books on Your Shelf
Here's a quick and simple tip to add simplicity to your life.

Most people have books in their home, including some books they haven't read yet. Make a deal with yourself to not buy any more books until you read the ones you have. If there are books you find you don't actually want to read, pass them along to others. After you read each book, decide if you want to keep it or pass it along.

GARAGE SALES AND CHARITIES

It's always better to find a use for an object, even an object you no longer need, than to simply throw it out. Of course, some things will have to be discarded, but for everything else you can find ways to help others using the possessions you are getting rid of.

You can have a garage sale, which is a way to make a little money with what you no longer need. I've done that a few times, and it's been nice to have a little extra cash.

But garage sales take a lot of time and effort, so these days, I tend to call a worthy, verified charity to come and pick up bags and boxes of my unwanted things. It blesses them with things they can reuse or sell, and it blesses me with the knowledge that what was once mine is now helping others.

Try This—Make Your Own

Whenever you go shopping, before you buy something first ask yourself if you truly need this item. Second, ask yourself if you can make it instead.

Asking those two simple questions—do I need it, and can I make it instead—will create a lot of simplicity and joy in your life. You may not be able to make everything, but making even just a few things will be a blessing to you.

SIMPLICITY SAVES MONEY AND TIME

When you begin simplifying your life, you'll enjoy some wonderful side effects. Since you are buying only what you really need, you will be saving money. Another benefit is that having less stuff means it's easier to keep your house and office clean, which saves you time. Less stuff and more space means more mental and emotional freedom as well.

Try This—Sobriety

Before I made simplicity a value that I wanted to express daily in my life, I spent a lot of time and money going out, drinking a lot, and using my credit cards on things I didn't really need.

But as my life changed and my values shifted, I found that being more sober in my thoughts, words, and actions created a much simpler life. It was more deliberate, with more meaning and less fluff. Simplicity doesn't mean a dull, boring life. For me, it means a life of joy, filled with authentic experiences.

Simplicity is the ultimate
sophistication.

—**LEONARDO DA VINCI**

HIDING BEHIND A CREDIT CARD

An emotional benefit to simplifying your life is that you no longer need to buy "things" to avoid emotional issues. This can be scary if you aren't prepared for it. Understand that when you feel bad and automatically turn to a little "retail therapy," you're avoiding something that needs attention now.

Instead of shopping (or drinking, or smoking, or whatever), make an effort to deal with what needs your attention. Once you do, the impulse to buy (or drink, or smoke, etc.) is lessened or just goes away. It makes things simple.

Try This—How Many Days Can I Go Without Buying Something?

In my quest for simplicity, I try to find ways to make it a game. One game I've played a few times involves seeing how many days I can go without buying anything new.

I set up certain exceptions, such as food and public transportation. Then I try to go as many days as I can without purchasing anything. I originally did this out of necessity, because I was broke. Later I did it because I wanted to live a simpler lifestyle.

Instead of adding more "things" to my life, I saved money, and I lived my value of simplicity.

5 WAYS TO KNOW YOU ARE LIVING A SIMPLER LIFE

You only want what you truly need.

Your home and your mind are free from clutter.

You choose to reuse and repurpose as much as possible.

You have more energy.

You don't experience constant complications.

WHO ARE YOU
WITHOUT YOUR STUFF?

It seems like every year we read about fires in places like California and Australia and elsewhere. These fires devastate so much, from wilderness to animals, and leave many people homeless in their wake. I can't imagine how difficult it would be to lose everything, even your home.

It also makes me wonder how I would react to that situation if I ever faced it. Imagine for yourself, and then ask yourself this question: Who would you be if you didn't have anything? How much of your identity is based on what you own?

Try This—Refuse to Use Plastic

Simple life means simple values. One of those values is to use as little plastic as possible. There are great uses for plastic, but just a quick walk through the aisles of a grocery store, or a store of almost any kind, shows just how much plastic is used unnecessarily, often for cosmetic reasons.

I once bought a small snack and discovered that it was wrapped in plastic, was sitting on a plastic tray that was inside a larger plastic tray, and was in a box that had a plastic film window to see the item inside.

It took me two minutes to eat—but for how many years will we see the impact of that plastic? Multiply that by millions of items, every single day, and it's mind-boggling. One act of simplicity is to use as little plastic as you possibly can, and another is to reuse the plastic you already have.

EXPERIENCE OVER OWNERSHIP

One of my friends travels a great deal. She takes trips around the world, and takes many photographs on her phone. When she returns from a trip, she looks at the photos she took in that country or area, and then picks only one from each that encapsulates the experience she had there.

She prints out that one photograph and hangs it on the wall. It's so simple, and yet so effective. When you go to her house and see those photographs, you can feel her experience. Experience is more valuable than ownership.

It is always the simple that produces the marvelous.

—AMELIA BARR